WAR: MAN'S ABYSMAL ABYSS-PLUNGE

THE WORKS OF SRI CHINMOY

WAR:
MAN'S ABYSMAL ABYSS-PLUNGE

★

LYON · OXFORD
GANAPATI PRESS
XCII

ISBN 978-1-911319-47-4

FIRST EDITION WENT TO PRESS ON 31 FEBRUARY 2023

WAR: MAN'S ABYSMAL ABYSS-PLUNGE

War is
The most nourishing food
For the senile.

War is
Man's self-exposed
Stupidity.

War is
Man's self-imposed
Futility.

War-story:
Stupidity fights.
Futility wins.

War
Is life's fastest
Backward march.

War
Is ignorance-slavery.

War
Is treasured
By ignorance-princes.

War
Is ego's self-made
Crown and throne.

War
Is complete and unconditional
Surrender to ignorance-forces.

War
Is the glad acceptance
Of destruction-invitation.

War
Is the destruction-discovery
Of the stupidity-mind.

Now
Is the only time
To end any war.

War
Is the mind's
Stark impurity-dance.

War broadcasts
The stupendous victory
Of Satan.

War compels
The heart's wisdom-light
To surrender to
The mind's stupidity-night.

War
Is the mind-temptation
Within
And life-destruction
Without.

War
Is the undivine confidence-presence
Of the hostile forces in man.

War
Is man's instigation-story
And not God's Inspiration-Song.

War
Is a self-styled stranger
To God's Compassion-Eye.

War
Is the greatest victory
Of inconscience-night.

War
Is world-possession-greed-
satisfaction.

War wants to prove
That the human mind
Has no greatness
And that the human heart
Has no goodness.

War invites
War-lovers
To come and participate
In a destruction-dance.

War
Is the joint
Elephant-madness
Of supremacy-hungry nations.

War
Is the irresistible sadness
Of the universal heart.

War
Is the utter disgrace-failure
Of the hostile minds.

War says:
"O man-made Compassion-God,
Where are You?"
God-made God-Peace answers:
"Shut up, you villain!
I am sleeplessly sick of you
And I am breathlessly
Disgusted with you."

In the inner world
War-mongers are
Pitiful fear-hostages.

Man's familiar war-excuse:
I was not responsible.
He, only he.

A man of war
Does not actually need anything
But wants everything immediately.

Alas, the heart
Cannot understand
Why and how
The mind's war-insanity
Is escalating.

We do not need
Heaven-born saints
But just earth-born seekers
Who believe in peace
And want to live in peace.

War-mongers are first-class
Insecurity-coward-singers.

He who loves war
Is undoubtedly
The abysmal terrorist.

God-lovers long for
Ever-advancing peace.
War-lovers desire
Ever-multiplying destruction.

A war-lover,
No matter how long
He chases after satisfaction-deer,
Will never succeed.

It is the height of absurdity
When the war-mongers interpret
In their own way
God's all-fulfilling Peace-Delight.

No human stupidity
Can take the place
Of the animal brutality:
War.

War enjoys
Helplessness-cries.
Peace enjoys
Fulness-smiles.

A man of war thinks
It is beneath his dignity
To visit a mental asylum
Although he is absolutely
The perfect patient.

War is the victory-drum
Of the animal consciousness.

War is the stupid winner
Of futility
And the unavoidable loser
Of dignity.

A man of war is, indeed,
The worst possible
Self-doubt-sufferer.

A man of war
Does not care for his heart
As long as he knows that
He has a world-devouring mind.

War is at once
Mind the thief
And heart the grief.

War shows me
The utter helplessness of earth
And the shocking indifference
Of Heaven.

War-enjoyers cannot answer
The simplest question,
Which any child can:
"What is life?"

A man of war
Has the face of shameless pride
And the heart of deathless insecurity.

War is man's
Mind-prison-slavery.

A war-monger is destined
To be a sorrow-millionaire.
A peace-lover eventually becomes
A joy-billionaire.

In the inner world
War-lovers are
Insecurity-dancers.

War-mongers do not respond
Even to God's
Urgent emergency Calls.

War-lovers are never permitted
To enter into the heart-kingdom.

War is man's
God-Satisfaction-promise-devourer.

APPENDIX

BIBLIOGRAPHY

Sri Chinmoy:

— War: man's abysmal abyss-plunge, part 1, Agni Press, 1991.
— War: man's abysmal abyss-plunge, part 2, Agni Press, 1991.

TABLE OF CONTENTS

War: man's abysmal abyss-plunge